Quarto is the authority on a wide range of topics.

Quarto educates, entertains and enriches the lives of our readers—enthusiasts and lovers of hands-on living.

www.quartoknows.com

First published in 2016 by Cool Springs Press, an imprint of Quarto Publishing Group USA Inc., 400 First Avenue North, Suite 400, Minneapolis, MN 55401 USA. Telephone: (612) 344-8100 Fax: (612) 344-8692

quartoknows.com
Visit our blogs at quartoknows.com

Cool Springs Press titles are also available at discounts in bulk quantity for industrial or sales-promotional use. For details contact the Special Sales Manager at Quarto Publishing Group USA Inc., 400 First Avenue North, Suite 400, Minneapolis, MN 55401 USA.

10 9 8 7 6 5 4 3 2 1

ISBN: 978-1-59186-678-7

Acquiring Editor: Mark Johanson
Project Manager: Alyssa Bluhm
Art Director: Brad Springer
Cover Design: Amelia LeBarron
Interior Design and Layout: Rebecca Pagel

Photo credits: Mandeville-King Seed Company of Rochester New York (Genesee County): 12, 41, 49, 65, 127
US Department of Agriculture: 16–17

Printed in China

GARDEN JOURNAL

MY PLANTING HISTORY, SUCCESSES & IDEAS

COOL SPRINGS PRESS

Home and Garden Experts™

MINNEAPOLIS, MINNESOTA

Contents

How to Use This Book

This durable, easy-to-use book is designed to give you the space to document all the important information for your vegetable or flower garden over several years. Each section is intended to evolve just like your gardening skills and experiences evolve over time. Following a brief introduction to some of the very basic sun and soil requirements for successful gardening, the remaining sections of the book will be completed gradually over time as you document your experiences with new plants, as you revise your garden spaces, and as you encounter new pests or new disease problems and record your treatment of them.

This is a book to jump around in, entering information here and there, and referring back whenever you need to refresh yourself on recent history. So get familiar with its organization. The book begins with a place to simply sketch a rough diagram of your yard and home site, documenting where your major trees are located, where driveways and walkways fall, and where your home and garage are located on the site. This can be helpful as you consider where you'd like to place new flower or vegetable garden beds in the future. Next is a section in which you can map out your garden planting areas, either to document as they currently exist, or to experiment with new layouts for the next season.

This is followed by a long month-by-month section where you can document various garden observations and details as they unfold over the course of the year. A short paragraph or two every year that summarizes what happens each month eventually creates a complete picture of your month-by-month gardening experiences and routines.

Next is a section for documenting the new plant varieties you may try, followed by sections to record the various insect pests and diseases that may affect your garden. There is also a section to put photos of your garden to record its evolution over time. And the book has pages that allow you to document the garden tools and various garden chemicals and products you use. The book closes with a place to log various garden resources, such as lawn services, garden centers, and university agriculture departments, and several blank pages to add notes on anything not covered elsewhere. Two convenient pockets in the back of the book give you space to store things such as seeds saved from favorite plants, news clippings of interesting garden articles, or the plastic plant ID stakes from the most recent year's planting choices—anything you find relevant to your gardening.

This is meant to be a hardworking book, so don't feel afraid to mark up it up, to staple notes into the pages, to sketch drawings on the provided pages or in the margins. Used successfully, it should become a ragtag, heavily used book that really shows its wear. *The Cool Springs Garden Journal* will quickly become one of your most important gardening tools.

Gardening Basics

It's simple: Gardening is fun and rewarding, whether you prefer growing your own edibles or would rather be a landscape artist by focusing on flowers and other ornamentals. There's nothing like going out in the evening to pick greens, cucumbers, and tomatoes for a salad, or strolling through the garden in the morning with a cup of coffee and cutting flowers for a table bouquet. Being a successful gardener takes practice, patience, and a good memory. Even the best, most experienced gardener is always learning. We can't help you with the first two, but we can help you remember what worked, what didn't, and what to do differently next year. *The Cool Springs Garden Journal* is the perfect tool to help you keep track of what's going on in your garden year after year.

To get started, here are some basics of gardening to guide you in the right direction. Then it's up to you to experiment with planting schemes, new varieties, and safe pest control techniques to make your garden productive, beautiful, and a statement of who you are. Let's take a look at each one.

SITE

Ideally, you'd have a garden location in full sun on great soil. But we all can't be so fortunate, so besides the sun and soil, what other factors are important in locating your vegetable garden? It's best to locate your vegetable plots or garden beds where you'll be able to see and check them regularly and not forget about them. Also, consider the water source. Is there a spigot close by? Do you need hoses to water the entire garden? Will you have to drag hoses through the garden to water? Having quick and easy access to water is critical to success.

Think of the area in terms of its other uses. Do you have kids and animals that will be running and playing in this spot? Is there an easy way to fence off the garden so it doesn't get trampled? Do you entertain, and will guests be walking in this area? Imagine how your garden will fit in the flow of the yard.

Once you understand the uses of your yard, then it's time to get down to the nitty-gritty of sun and soil.

SUNLIGHT

Understanding the light in your garden will help you determine which plants will thrive in which locations. It's also important to consider how sunlight falls in your garden at different times of day and at different times of the year.

It's common knowledge that most plants grow best in full sun, but it's a little more involved than just finding the sunniest spot in your yard to grow a garden. Full sun generally means at least six hours of direct sun a day. It can be broken up with some hours in the morning and some in the afternoon, but the total needs to be at least six, especially for sun-loving flowers or fruiting crops such as

tomatoes, squash, cucumbers, beans, and peppers. If you have the perfect location and you notice it only gets three to four hours of direct sun a day, you still can grow many flowers and some vegetables. You'll just have to stick with those that can take less direct light.

Even if you find you only have 1 to 2 hours of direct sun a day, you still can grow some flowers, vegetables, and herbs. Your edibles palette is more limited, but you can grow leafy greens such as kale, parsley, spinach, lettuce, and arugula in this shadier location. Of course, these and the root crops will produce better in full sun, but the point is that they will still survive to yield a harvest. Flower gardeners will find that hostas, impatiens, and many other ornamentals will still grow in mostly shady locations.

SOIL

After you find a location with the most sun possible, take a good look at the soil. The soil is the soul of the garden. If you feed it well, it will feed your plants and you'll have plentiful flowers and vegetables every year. The first step is to see what type of soil you have. Dig down and feel the soil. If it mostly feels slimy and slippery, it's probably dominated by clay. If it mostly feels gritty, it's probably mostly sand. If it has a little of both, it's probably loam. Clay is fertile and holds water well, but it's hard to work; anyone who has clay soil feels it looks like concrete when it dries out. Sand is easy to work, but it doesn't hold water (think of the beach!) or nutrients well. Loam is the happy middle, so it is the most desirable soil to have.

Whatever soil you have, adding organic matter will help make it better. Organic matter comes in many forms, such as compost, composted manure, untreated grass clippings,

straw, and chopped leaves. It provides food for the microbes in the soil, which help make nutrients and water available for plant roots. If you have a great spot but the soil seems to have too much clay or sand, don't give up. Think about adding compost and other organic matter materials in abundance to make it healthier.

For the best growth, the soil acidity (or pH) should be between 6.5 and 7.2. Based on a soil test, add lime to raise the pH or sulfur to lower it to this range. You can also use the test results to add other nutrients, such as phosphorus, magnesium, and potassium, as needed.

Finally, check the soil for its water drainage. Dig a hole 1 foot wide by 1 foot deep, fill it with water, and wait. If the water takes longer than eight hours to drain, you have a water drainage problem and should move to a better-drained site or grow on raised beds.

WATER

Watering is the most important task in the garden and the one most often done improperly. Watering is something that most gardeners enjoy doing because it makes us feel like we're accomplishing something. We see a plant that has wilted, we water it, and it perks up. Job well done! But doing this kind of "rescue" watering is just one of gardeners' several bad watering habits. The biggest watering mistake of all—whether watering by hand or with the assistance of an automatic irrigation system—is watering too frequently and shallowly instead of giving the ground a thorough and deep soaking that will sustain plants for several days or more without needing to be watered again.

In a nutshell, shallow watering makes for shallow roots. When roots reside in the top few inches of the soil, they dry out very quickly

10

and demand more water. You find yourself returning over and over, day after day, to water the same plants you watered the day before. Instead, watering thoroughly and deeply when you water will encourage a plant's roots to grow deep into the soil, seeking out moisture as they grow. Then, even in times of intense heat or extended drought, plants are better equipped to survive because their roots reach deep into the cooler soil where more water is available.

TEMPERATURE

Gardeners are most interested in temperature because of how it relates to a plant's cold hardiness. This is especially true of perennial garden flowers, for which hardiness means the plant's ability to survive the winter and emerge again the following spring. You can determine your hardiness zone by consulting a USDA Hardiness Zone Map (like the one on pages 16-17) and finding where your home and garden lie within a certain range based on the coldest average winter temperatures in your region. If you garden in Zone 5, then every plant you grow and want to survive the winter must be hardy to at least that zone. Plants that are hardy to Zone 3 (two zones colder) will also grow in Zone 5, because their minimum temperature tolerance is even lower, while plants that are only hardy to Zone 7 (two zones warmer) will probably not survive the cold temperatures of a Zone 5 winter.

Heat tolerance also comes into play with certain plants and in certain regions of the country. For instance, gardeners in the South and Southwest will find limited success with many plants that are native to the mild, maritime climate of the Pacific Northwest. They simply can't withstand the brutal heat and humidity

of a southern summer or the sizzling climate of the desert.

Understanding both cold hardiness and heat tolerance is an enormous advantage when planning and planting your flower gardens, whether it's with annual and perennial garden flowers or with flowering shrubs and trees.

SIZE

Small is beautiful for a beginning garden lover. There's nothing more encouraging than success in the garden, and it's better to be successful at growing a few rose bushes or a small row of bush beans and some lettuce than to be overwhelmed by all that's involved in a huge garden.

And you can still garden even if you don't have beds in the ground. The most efficient

bark mulch, or chopped leaves. These materials will prevent weeds from growing, maintain the soil moisture, and make for easier walking.

If you don't have room for raised beds, container gardening is a snap. Look for self-watering containers with a water reservoir in the bottom. These allow you to fill the reservoir and go away, even for days, without having to worry about plants drying out. Self-watering containers come as window boxes, hanging baskets, railing planters, and on-the-ground containers. Some are even big enough to grow full-sized tomato plants. The beauty of containers is that you can move them to protect the plants from frost, wind, and animals, or to expose them to more sun or shade, depending on the need.

Give your plants enough room to grow too. Small flowering perennials can become massive in a short time. Look at the types of vegetables you're growing and imagine how much space they will take up. Tomatoes can grow 6 feet tall or more, dominating the landscape. Make sure every plant type has enough room to grow its best.

way to grow vegetables is in raised beds (raised beds are also wonderful for flower gardeners with mobility issues). Raised beds can be formed by mounding up the soil into 3- to 4-foot-wide, 8-inch-high rows that are flat on top. You'll have to create the bed each year, as it will naturally flatten over time. A more permanent method is to make raised beds with rot-resistant woods (such as cedar or redwood), pavers, stone, or cement blocks. These materials keep the bed raised for years. Make either type of bed no more than 4 feet wide so you can reach into the center of the bed without ever stepping on it. This will avoid compacting the soil. Raised beds drain water, heat up faster in spring, and allow you to concentrate on weeding, watering, and feeding in a smaller space without wasting any of these resources on pathways. You can make the raised beds any shape you like, such as rectangular, square, round, or octagonal, as long as they don't get wider than 4 feet. Between the raised beds, consider mulching the paths with newspaper, cardboard, straw, untreated grass clippings,

SELECTION

Growing the best types of flowers and vegetables will help you be successful in your garden. The first point is almost too obvious: Grow what you like to eat and what you find attractive. Some vegetable gardeners grow vegetables they think they should grow but may not like to eat, such as beans. Some flower

gardeners grow roses because they think it's somehow "expected," not because they really like them. Make sure to grow what you genuinely enjoy.

When planning your garden, consider the orientation of the sun. Plant tall plants on the north side and short plants on the south side so that the short ones won't be in the shade. If you're vegetable gardening, grow the right vegetables at the right time for your area. Cool-weather-loving vegetables, such as spinach, lettuce, carrots, beets, cabbage, broccoli, peas, and kale, should be planted in spring to mature before the heat of summer or planted in late summer to mature during the cooler weather of fall (or winter in a warmer climate). Warm-weather-loving vegetables, such as tomatoes, peppers, eggplant, beans, squash, cucumber, melons, and sweet potatoes, should be planted after all danger of frost has passed to grow and mature during the heat of summer. Your local Master Gardener group or extension service should have a planting schedule for your area that will help you know when to plant various vegetables.

VARIETIES

Both flowers and vegetables are available in many different varieties, and the available selections will change rapidly. Home garden vegetables are usually classified as heirlooms or hybrids. Heirlooms are generally defined as any vegetables bred before World War II. They're open pollinated, meaning that if you save the seed properly, you can grow the same variety the next year (and get a plant that is identical to the parent plant). Heirlooms are fascinating, delicious, and unique. Take tomatoes, for example. There are heirloom tomatoes in almost every color of the rainbow, from black to white. They come in a variety of fruit flavors and plant shapes; some grow like fir trees, while others have strawberry-shaped fruits. However, heirlooms were bred in very specific regions of the country and the world, so they aren't universally adapted to all growing areas. When trying heirlooms in your garden, consider checking out the varieties that your friends, local growers, and regional seed companies have found successful in their trials. These should do well in your garden too.

Hybrids were developed in the 1950s and dominate the market. They aren't generally as varied as heirlooms, but what they lack in creativity they make up for in consistency. Hybrids are varieties that were crossed a number of different times to acquire desired traits. These traits might be productivity, disease resistance, or fruit firmness. If you save hybrid seeds, they won't come "true to type." You'll get a whole range of growth characteristics, some good and some not. Hybrid varieties can grow across the country and produce just about the same wherever they're planted. Some vegetables, such as tomatoes and sweet corn, are dominated by hybrids, while other vegetables, such as lettuce and peas, are open-pollinated varieties. Consider growing some heirloom and some hybrid varieties in your garden to see which perform the best and which you like to eat.

Whatever variety you grow, be sure to harvest at the proper time for that variety. Overly mature produce may rot on the vine or become so large it's inedible. Plus, if the plants form mature seeds, they stop producing, so you get less output. If you have an abundance of produce, make more friends by giving away

TURNIP
RUTABAGA

·CARD SEED CO·
FREDONIA, N.Y.

FEEDING YOUR GARDEN

Caring for your soil by adding compost, manures, and other high-quality organic material is one of the best ways to have a healthy garden. When you care for your soil, your garden plants will need only an occasional boost in the form of an annual application of a slow-acting, all-purpose fertilizer to keep them in top shape. Today, many gardeners are leaning toward all-natural and organic fertilizers in their quest to be more earth friendly.

Whether you choose to go the organic route or to use a synthetic chemical fertilizer, the product will show a three-number series on the package that is important for you to understand.

This number, 10-10-10 for instance, will be listed on the package label and indicates the percentages of the three major nutrients—nitrogen, phosphorus, and potassium—that the fertilizer in that package contains. In this example, 10 percent of the contents of the bag is nitrogen, 10 percent is phosphorus, and 10 percent is potassium. The remaining ingredients are the carriers that deliver the nutrients to the soil and eventually to the plants. Many fertilizers will have trace amounts of other nutrients that plants also need to grow properly, but in such small amounts that they are often not listed individually on the package. Just know that they are there and filling an important role in your garden. Some flowering plants, especially annuals and a few perennials that flower almost continually (or at least for an extended period of time), may need supplemental feeding during the summer. This can come either in the form of a second application of dry, granular fertilizer later in the season or as a liquid fertilizer that can be applied periodically when watering.

fresh vegetables or consider preserving them. Canning tomatoes, making pickles, and freezing beans are good ways to have the tastes of summer all winter long.

Plant varieties are just as plentiful for flower gardeners, where the motivation for professional growers is to create varieties with unique new colors, sizes, or looks, or with new characteristics such as resistance to pests or diseases. Some plants, like daylilies, may have many hundreds of varieties available, with dozens more introduced each year. Paying attention to seed and plant catalogue retailers is the best way to stay abreast of what is newest and best in the world of ornamental varieties. A plant species that was of average garden appeal last year may suddenly have new varieties that make your mouth water.

A WORD ABOUT PESTS

An introduction to gardening wouldn't be complete without a word about pests. Even gardens with the healthiest soil that are well tended and protected will eventually run into problems with diseases, insects, or animals. It's always best to use sprays, even organic ones, as a last resort. Before spraying, properly identify the problem. You'll be surprised how weather can cause symptoms that look like some diseases and insects. Look to grow resistant varieties to avoid the problem. For example, 'Defiant' and 'Mountain Magic' are two tomato varieties that are resistant to early and late blight diseases. 'King Hairy' potato resists Colorado potato beetle attacks.

Consider barriers to prevent insects or animals from finding your plants. A good fence will keep out rabbits and deer, floating row covers will prevent cabbageworms from laying eggs on cabbage-family crops, and strips of newspaper wrapped around pepper or tomato stems will prevent cutworms from chopping down your transplant. Yellow sticky traps will draw cucumber beetles away from cucumbers and squash. Beer traps will lure snails and slugs away from hostas and lettuce. Gathering or crushing squash bug eggs or Japanese beetle adults can be a way to reduce the damage too.

If you must spray, always do so following the label directions and use targeted organic sprays, such as *Bacillus thuringiensis* (Bt, DiPel, Thuricide) first. This pesticide only attacks caterpillar-family pests, such as cabbageworms and tomato hornworm, and isn't harmful to pets, wildlife, or humans.

WRITING IT DOWN

One of the key ways to keep your garden healthy year after year is to remember what worked and didn't work in the previous years. The best way to remember is to write it down. Having a month-by-month garden journal allows you to highlight weather conditions, planting dates, dates when pests appeared, harvest dates, and, most important, the varieties, plant combinations, and techniques that worked well in your garden. Your garden journal becomes a living history of the progress in your garden, as well as a place to jot down what you're thinking.

USDA Plant Hardiness Zone Map

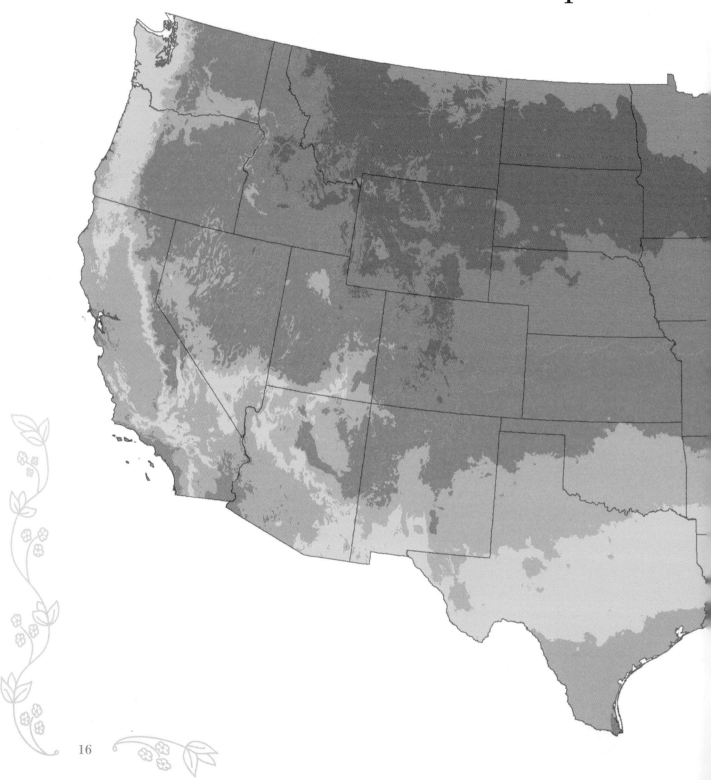

Average Annual Extreme Minimum Temperature 1976-2005

Temp (F)	Zone	Temp (C)
-60 to -50	1	-51.1 to -45.6
-50 to -40	2	-45.6 to -40
-40 to -30	3	-40 to -34.4
-30 to -20	4	-34.4 to -28.9
-20 to -10	5	-28.9 to -23.3
-10 to 0	6	-23.3 to -17.8
0 to 10	7	-17.8 to -12.2
10 to 20	8	-12.2 to -6.7
20 to 30	9	-6.7 to -1.1
30 to 40	10	-1.1 to 4.4
40 to 50	11	4.4 to 10
50 to 60	12	10 to 15.6
60 to 70	13	15.6 to 21.1

Site Map

Use these gridded pages to sketch out your property, showing where the house and
other buildings are located, and where permanent features such as trees, walkways,
patios, and fences are located. Check with local utility companies and mark down the
location of underground utility lines, such as electrical and gas service, sewer and water
lines, and cable television and other utilities. This can be a helpful diagram to use
when planning the location of garden planting areas.

Address of property: _____

Legal description: _____

Overall dimensions of lot: _____

My Garden Maps

These gridded pages can be used to either map your existing garden areas, keeping track year-by-year of what you've planted and where, or to test out new or revised garden arrangements. If you need more space, use tissue paper, photocopies of the grid pages, or additional graph paper to create more sketches.

My Garden Maps

My Garden Maps

Monthly Garden Notes

January

No occupation is **so delightful** to me
as the culture of the earth, and no culture comparable
to that of the garden. . . . But though an old man,
I am but a young gardener.

—*Thomas Jefferson*

Tip: Plant catalogs will begin arriving early in the year to entice you with spectacular pictures and lavish descriptions of the newest and best plants for the coming garden season. Order early to ensure you get all the seeds and plants you want, because many will be in high demand and may sell out quickly. Now is the time to sketch out your garden on the grid pages in this journal to help you figure out how much space you have. Be sure to leave spaces in your sketch for any current empty space as well as for plants you might want to move somewhere else. Then use your catalogs to dream and plan what you order.

February

If you have a garden and a library,
you have everything you need.

—*Cicero*

34

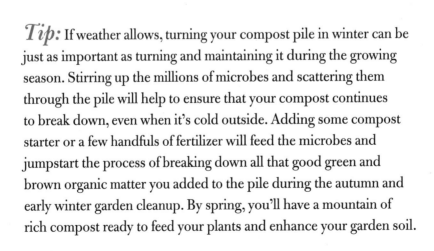

Tip: If weather allows, turning your compost pile in winter can be just as important as turning and maintaining it during the growing season. Stirring up the millions of microbes and scattering them through the pile will help to ensure that your compost continues to break down, even when it's cold outside. Adding some compost starter or a few handfuls of fertilizer will feed the microbes and jumpstart the process of breaking down all that good green and brown organic matter you added to the pile during the autumn and early winter garden cleanup. By spring, you'll have a mountain of rich compost ready to feed your plants and enhance your garden soil.

37

March

There is something **infinitely healing** in the repeated refrains of nature—the assurance that dawn comes after night, and spring after winter.

—*Rachel Carson*, Silent Spring

Tip: As soon as your soil has started to dry out and can be worked, amend it with compost for this spring growing season. Based on a soil test, consider adding other nutrients, minerals, and lime or sulfur to adjust the pH, especially if you're growing vegetables. Most plants grow best with a pH between 6.5 and 7.2. On healthy soil, add a 1- to 2-inch layer of compost and turn it under with these added nutrients. On poor soils, add a 3- to 4-inch layer of compost. Plant a week or so later.

April

Whan that Aprill with his shoures soote
The droghte of March hath perced to the roote
And bathed every veyne in swich licour,
Of which vertu engendred is the flour . . .

—*Geoffrey Chaucer,* The Canterbury Tales

43

Tip: As perennial plants begin to grow, consider if any need to be dug up and divided. Division can help control the size of plants that have grown too large for their space. It can also help improve their growth habits. Did you notice last year that some plants didn't seem as strong or sturdy as the year before? Did they flop over onto their neighbors? Did they flower less than usual? All of these could be signs that those plants are overcrowded and need dividing. Most perennials need to be divided every three to four years to keep them growing vigorously.

May

Don't judge each day by the harvest you reap,
but by the seeds you plant.

—*Robert Louis Stevenson*

Tip: Staking tall plants is a job that many gardeners forget, ignore, or think is too big a hassle. Staking is a huge benefit to many plants and, when done properly, can be a quick, easy, and painless job. The key to staking is to do it early—before the plants even need it! This is especially true for fall-blooming plants, as well as for summer-maturing flowers and vegetables. Staking in spring allows you to get between plants and to push the sticks or stakes into the ground where you need them. They'll only be visible for a few weeks before they are entirely hidden by the plants they're supporting.

June

The **best** fertilizer is the gardener's shadow.

—Proverb

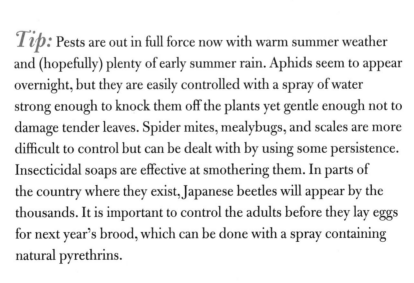

Tip: Pests are out in full force now with warm summer weather and (hopefully) plenty of early summer rain. Aphids seem to appear overnight, but they are easily controlled with a spray of water strong enough to knock them off the plants yet gentle enough not to damage tender leaves. Spider mites, mealybugs, and scales are more difficult to control but can be dealt with by using some persistence. Insecticidal soaps are effective at smothering them. In parts of the country where they exist, Japanese beetles will appear by the thousands. It is important to control the adults before they lay eggs for next year's brood, which can be done with a spray containing natural pyrethrins.

July

Heaven is **under our feet**
as well as **over** our heads.
—*Henry David Thoreau*, Walden

54

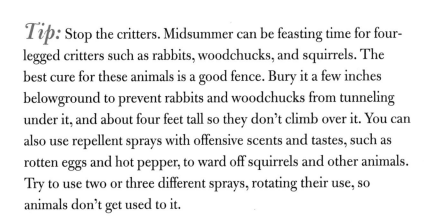

Tip: Stop the critters. Midsummer can be feasting time for four-legged critters such as rabbits, woodchucks, and squirrels. The best cure for these animals is a good fence. Bury it a few inches belowground to prevent rabbits and woodchucks from tunneling under it, and about four feet tall so they don't climb over it. You can also use repellent sprays with offensive scents and tastes, such as rotten eggs and hot pepper, to ward off squirrels and other animals. Try to use two or three different sprays, rotating their use, so animals don't get used to it.

August

The best place to seek God is
in the garden. You can dig for him there.
—*George Bernard Shaw*

Tip: Summertime means a lot of time spent in the garden weeding, watering, and maintaining what we've worked so hard to create. It also means taking care of yourself while you're outdoors. The sun comes up early in the summertime. Get out there with it! You can easily get in two to three hours of work before the sun is high enough to be unbearable. Drink plenty of water. Dehydration is serious business and you don't want to experience it! Be sure to wear your sunscreen, preferably a good waterproof brand that is at least SPF 30. And be sure to cover the back of your neck, your ears, and the back of your hands, in addition to the obvious places.

PEAS

PROUT'S SEED HOUSE
PIONEER GROWERS SEED AND PRODUCE
PORTAGE LA PRAIRIE · MANITOBA

September

If you wish to **be happy** for a week, kill a pig; if you wish to **be happy** for a month, get married; if you wish to **be happy** forever, make a garden.

—*Proverb*

Tip: Weeding is one of the most dreaded of garden tasks. Weeds are not only unsightly; they also steal valuable water and nutrients from the soil, often very efficiently. Fall weeds germinate rapidly during September, while the soil is still warm but air temperatures begin to drop. If you have maintained 1½ to 2 inches of mulch in your garden, weed growth should be minimal. Those that do come up can be pulled quickly and easily, often in as little as an hour or two a week. Never put weeds that have gone to seed in the compost pile, or you'll just redistribute the seeds when you use the compost.

October

The garden is the poor man's
apothecary.

—*Proverb*

Tip: Fall is the ideal time to plant trees and shrubs, giving them the chance to get their roots established before the ground freezes and a head start come spring when it's time to grow again. Planting at the proper depth is important! Dig a hole the same depth, but twice as wide, as the rootball and plant it at the same depth it was growing before. Fill in around the sides and pack the soil firmly enough to hold the plant in place, but not so tightly that you restrict root growth. Water deeply once a week as long as the ground is not frozen.

November

He who **plants** a garden
plants happiness.
—*Proverb*

Tip: If you haven't hung your birdfeeders, now's the time to get them out. Seeds with high fat content, such as black-oil sunflower and safflower, are especially good for maintaining birds' body fat and increasing their ability to stay warm when winter winds are cold and biting. You can even grow sunflowers in your summer garden, collect the dried seedheads, and hang them whole from your trees, allowing the birds to pick the seeds straight from the dried heads. Fresh water is also important for birds during the winter because many sources freeze over. Special heaters easily keep birdbaths thawed.

December

A **writer** is like a bean plant—
he has his day and then he gets **stringy**.

—*E.B. White*

Tip: Sow windowsill herbs, such as parsley, thyme, and chives, in containers now. They grow best in clay pots. In southern areas, these herbs will grow best in a sunny, south-facing window and produce well indoors by spring. In northern areas, the days are too short and light levels too low for proper growth, so consider placing a small grow light over them in the window. Keep the soil barely moist, because they won't be growing fast. Once germinated, check the herbs for any insects and spray with insecticidal soap to control them.

Yearly Garden Summaries

In this section, jot down a few paragraphs at the end of each year to summarize your garden experiences, creating a year-over-year story of your garden—what succeeded, what didn't, what the weather patterns were, what problems you encountered, what triumphs you enjoyed. You can create a small essay, telling the story of your garden for that year, or just use the space for informal notes. If you'd like, you can even insert a photo or two of that year's garden.

Year 1

Year 2

Year 3

Year 4

Year 5

Year 6

My Garden Plants

Use this section to document the various plants you try in your garden, their variety, where and when you planted them, where they came from and how much they cost, and what your experiences were.

Plant Species & Variety:

Planting Date:

Where Planted:

Source:

Cost:

Care Notes:

Animals and Insects Attracted:

Conclusions:

Plant Species & Variety:

Planting Date:

Where Planted:

Source:

Cost:

Care Notes:

Animals and Insects Attracted:

Conclusions:

Plant Species & Variety:

Planting Date:

Where Planted:

Source:

Cost:

Care Notes:

Animals and Insects Attracted:

Conclusions:

Plant Species & Variety:

Planting Date:

Where Planted:

Source:

Cost:

Care Notes:

Animals and Insects Attracted:

Conclusions:

Plant Species & Variety:

Planting Date:

Where Planted:

Source:

Cost:

Care Notes:

Animals and Insects Attracted:

Conclusions:

Plant Species & Variety:

Planting Date:

Where Planted:

Source:

Cost:

Care Notes:

Animals and Insects Attracted:

Conclusions:

Plant Species & Variety:

Planting Date:

Where Planted:

Source:

Cost:

Care Notes:

Animals and Insects Attracted:

Conclusions:

Plant Species & Variety:

Planting Date:

Where Planted:

Source:

Cost:

Care Notes:

Animals and Insects Attracted:

Conclusions:

Plant Species & Variety:

Planting Date:

Where Planted:

Source:

Cost:

Care Notes:

Animals and Insects Attracted:

Conclusions:

Plant Species & Variety:

Planting Date:

Where Planted:

Source:

Cost:

Care Notes:

Animals and Insects Attracted:

Conclusions:

Plant Species & Variety:

Planting Date:

Where Planted:

Source:

Cost:

Care Notes:

Animals and Insects Attracted:

Conclusions:

Plant Species & Variety:

Planting Date:

Where Planted:

Source:

Cost:

Care Notes:

Animals and Insects Attracted:

Conclusions:

Plant Species & Variety:

Planting Date:

Where Planted:

Source:

Cost:

Care Notes:

Animals and Insects Attracted:

Conclusions:

Plant Species & Variety:

Planting Date:

Where Planted:

Source:

Cost:

Care Notes:

Animals and Insects Attracted:

Conclusions:

Plant Species & Variety:

Planting Date:

Where Planted:

Source:

Cost:

Care Notes:

Animals and Insects Attracted:

Conclusions:

Plant Species & Variety:

Planting Date:

Where Planted:

Source:

Cost:

Care Notes:

Animals and Insects Attracted:

Conclusions:

Plant Species & Variety:

Planting Date:

Where Planted:

Source:

Cost:

Care Notes:

Animals and Insects Attracted:

Conclusions:

Plant Species & Variety:

Planting Date:

Where Planted:

Source:

Cost:

Care Notes:

Animals and Insects Attracted:

Conclusions:

Plant Species & Variety:

Planting Date:

Where Planted:

Source:

Cost:

Care Notes:

Animals and Insects Attracted:

Conclusions:

Plant Species & Variety:

Planting Date:

Where Planted:

Source:

Cost:

Care Notes:

Animals and Insects Attracted:

Conclusions:

Plant Species & Variety:

Planting Date:

Where Planted:

Source:

Cost:

Care Notes:

Animals and Insects Attracted:

Conclusions:

Plant Species & Variety:

Planting Date:

Where Planted:

Source:

Cost:

Care Notes:

Animals and Insects Attracted:

Conclusions:

Plant Species & Variety:

Planting Date:

Where Planted:

Source:

Cost:

Care Notes:

Animals and Insects Attracted:

Conclusions:

Plant Species & Variety:

Planting Date:

Where Planted:

Source:

Cost:

Care Notes:

Animals and Insects Attracted:

Conclusions:

Plant Species & Variety:

Planting Date:

Where Planted:

Source:

Cost:

Care Notes:

Animals and Insects Attracted:

Conclusions:

Plant Species & Variety:

Planting Date:

Where Planted:

Source:

Cost:

Care Notes:

Animals and Insects Attracted:

Conclusions:

Plant Species & Variety:

Planting Date:

Where Planted:

Source:

Cost:

Care Notes:

Animals and Insects Attracted:

Conclusions:

Plant Species & Variety:

Planting Date:

Where Planted:

Source:

Cost:

Care Notes:

Animals and Insects Attracted:

Conclusions:

My Garden Problems

Use these pages to keep track of problematic pests and diseases
that affect your garden, including when they attack, as well as what
treatments you used and how well they worked.

Pest or Disease:

Plants Affected:

Dates Appearing:

Treatments Tried:

Place photo of
pest or disease here.

Conclusions:

Pest or Disease:

Plants Affected:

Dates Appearing:

Treatments Tried:

Conclusions:

Pest or Disease:

Plants Affected:

Dates Appearing:

Treatments Tried:

Conclusions:

Pest or Disease:

Plants Affected:

Dates Appearing:

Treatments Tried:

Conclusions:

Pest or Disease:

Plants Affected:

Dates Appearing:

Treatments Tried:

Conclusions:

Pest or Disease:

Plants Affected:

Dates Appearing:

Treatments Tried:

Conclusions:

Pest or Disease:

Plants Affected:

Dates Appearing:

Treatments Tried:

Conclusions:

Pest or Disease:

Plants Affected:

Dates Appearing:

Treatments Tried:

Conclusions:

Pest or Disease:

Plants Affected:

Dates Appearing:

Treatments Tried:

Conclusions:

Pest or Disease:

Plants Affected:

Dates Appearing:

Treatments Tried:

Conclusions:

Pest or Disease:

Plants Affected:

Dates Appearing:

Treatments Tried:

Conclusions:

Pest or Disease:

Plants Affected:

Dates Appearing:

Treatments Tried:

Conclusions:

Pest or Disease:

Plants Affected:

Dates Appearing:

Treatments Tried:

Conclusions:

Pest or Disease:

Plants Affected:

Dates Appearing:

Treatments Tried:

Conclusions:

Pest or Disease:

Plants Affected:

Dates Appearing:

Treatments Tried:

Conclusions:

Pest or Disease:

Plants Affected:

Dates Appearing:

Treatments Tried:

Conclusions:

My Garden Photos

My Garden Photos

My Garden Photos

110

My Garden Photos

Garden Products I've Used

Use this section to document the various fertilizers, pesticides, herbicides, and other products you've used in your garden. List their sources, their cost, and their effectiveness.

Product:

Source:

Cost:

Used for:

Results:

Warnings:

Product:

Source:

Cost:

Used for:

Results:

Warnings:

Product:

Source:

Cost:

Used for:

Results:

Warnings:

Product:

Source:

Cost:

Used for:

Results:

Warnings:

My Garden Gear

Here's a place to keep track of the trowels, shovels, rakes,
pruners, and any other tools or hardware you own.

Tool	Source & Cost	Loaned out? To?

Tool	Source & Cost	Loaned out? To?

Garden Resources

These pages offer a place to keep track of your local garden business and resources, such as lawn services, garden centers, arborists and tree pruners, garden clubs, and university extension services. You can also list national resources, such as garden seed suppliers and online garden magazines.

Name of Resource:

Description:

Website, Email, Telephone:

Comments:

Name of Resource:

Description:

Website, Email, Telephone:

Comments:

Name of Resource:

Description:

Website, Email, Telephone:

Comments:

Name of Resource:

Description:

Website, Email, Telephone:

Comments:

Name of Resource:

Description:

Website, Email, Telephone:

Comments:

Name of Resource:

Description:

Website, Email, Telephone:

Comments:

Name of Resource:

Description:

Website, Email, Telephone:

Comments:

Notes

Notes